Official SQA Past Papers WITH ANSWERS

Intermediate 2
Units 1, 2 and 3
Mathematics
2010–2014

HODDER GIBSON
AN HACHETTE UK COMPANY

CW00631413

Hodder Gibson is grateful to the copyright holders, as credited on the final page of the Question Section, for permission to use their material. Every effort has been made to trace the copyright holders and to obtain their permission for the use of copyright material. Hodder Gibson will be happy to receive information allowing us to rectify any error or omission in future editions.

Hachette UK's policy is to use papers that are natural, renewable and recyclable products and made from wood grown in sustainable forests. The logging and manufacturing processes are expected to conform to the environmental regulations of the country of origin.

Orders: please contact Bookpoint Ltd, 130 Park Drive, Abingdon, Oxon OX14 4SE. Telephone: (44) 01235 827720. Fax: (44) 01235 400454.

Lines are open 9.00–5.00, Monday to Saturday, with a 24-hour message answering service. Visit our website at www.hoddereducation.co.uk. Hodder Gibson can be contacted direct on: Tel: 0141 848 1609; Fax: 0141 889 6315; email: hoddergibson@hodder.co.uk

This collection first published in 2014 by

Hodder Gibson, an imprint of Hodder Education,

An Hachette UK Company

2a Christie Street

Paisley PA1 1NB

{BrightRED   Hodder Gibson is grateful to Bright Red Publishing Ltd for collaborative work in preparation of this book and all SQA Past Paper, National 5 and CfE Higher Model Paper titles 2014.

Past Papers © Scottish Qualifications Authority. Answers and Study Skills section © Hodder Gibson. All rights reserved.
Apart from any use permitted under UK copyright law, no part of this publication may be reproduced or transmitted in any form or by any means, electronic or mechanical, including photocopying and recording, or held within any information storage and retrieval system, without permission in writing from the publisher or under licence from the Copyright Licensing Agency Limited.
Further details of such licences (for reprographic reproduction) may be obtained from the Copyright Licensing Agency Limited, Saffron House, 6–10 Kirby Street, London EC1N 8TS.

Typeset by PDQ Digital Media Solutions Ltd, Bungay, Suffolk NR35 1BY

Printed in the UK

A catalogue record for this title is available from the British Library

ISBN 978-1-4718-3692-3

3 2 1

2015 2014

Introduction

Study Skills – what you need to know to pass exams!

Pause for thought

Many students might skip quickly through a page like this. After all, we all know how to revise. Do you really though?

Think about this:

"IF YOU ALWAYS DO WHAT YOU ALWAYS DO, YOU WILL ALWAYS GET WHAT YOU HAVE ALWAYS GOT."

Do you like the grades you get? Do you want to do better? If you get full marks in your assessment, then that's great! Change nothing! This section is just to help you get that little bit better than you already are.

There are two main parts to the advice on offer here. The first part highlights fairly obvious things but which are also very important. The second part makes suggestions about revision that you might not have thought about but which WILL help you.

Part 1

DOH! It's so obvious but …

Start revising in good time

Don't leave it until the last minute – this will make you panic.

Make a revision timetable that sets out work time AND play time.

Sleep and eat!

Obvious really, and very helpful. Avoid arguments or stressful things too – even games that wind you up. You need to be fit, awake and focused!

Know your place!

Make sure you know exactly **WHEN and WHERE** your exams are.

Know your enemy!

Make sure you know what to expect in the exam.

How is the paper structured?

How much time is there for each question?

What types of question are involved?

Which topics seem to come up time and time again?

Which topics are your strongest and which are your weakest?

Are all topics compulsory or are there choices?

Learn by DOING!

There is no substitute for past papers and practice papers – they are simply essential! Tackling this collection of papers and answers is exactly the right thing to be doing as your exams approach.

Part 2

People learn in different ways. Some like low light, some bright. Some like early morning, some like evening / night. Some prefer warm, some prefer cold. But everyone uses their BRAIN and the brain works when it is active. Passive learning – sitting gazing at notes – is the most INEFFICIENT way to learn anything. Below you will find tips and ideas for making your revision more effective and maybe even more enjoyable. What follows gets your brain active, and active learning works!

Activity 1 – Stop and review

Step 1

When you have done no more than 5 minutes of revision reading STOP!

Step 2

Write a heading in your own words which sums up the topic you have been revising.

Step 3

Write a summary of what you have revised in no more than two sentences. Don't fool yourself by saying, "I know it, but I cannot put it into words". That just means you don't know it well enough. If you cannot write your summary, revise that section again, knowing that you must write a summary at the end of it. Many of you will have notebooks full of blue/black ink writing. Many of the pages will not be especially attractive or memorable so try to liven them up a bit with colour as you are reviewing and rewriting. **This is a great memory aid, and memory is the most important thing.**

Activity 2 — Use technology!

Why should everything be written down? Have you thought about "mental" maps, diagrams, cartoons and colour to help you learn? And rather than write down notes, why not record your revision material?

What about having a text message revision session with friends? Keep in touch with them to find out how and what they are revising and share ideas and questions.

Why not make a video diary where you tell the camera what you are doing, what you think you have learned and what you still have to do? No one has to see or hear it, but the process of having to organise your thoughts in a formal way to explain something is a very important learning practice.

Be sure to make use of electronic files. You could begin to summarise your class notes. Your typing might be slow, but it will get faster and the typed notes will be easier to read than the scribbles in your class notes. Try to add different fonts and colours to make your work stand out. You can easily Google relevant pictures, cartoons and diagrams which you can copy and paste to make your work more attractive and **MEMORABLE**.

Activity 3 – This is it. Do this and you will know lots!

Step 1

In this task you must be very honest with yourself! Find the SQA syllabus for your subject (www.sqa.org.uk). Look at how it is broken down into main topics called MANDATORY knowledge. That means stuff you MUST know.

Step 2

BEFORE you do ANY revision on this topic, write a list of everything that you already know about the subject. It might be quite a long list but you only need to write it once. It shows you all the information that is already in your long-term memory so you know what parts you do not need to revise!

Step 3

Pick a chapter or section from your book or revision notes. Choose a fairly large section or a whole chapter to get the most out of this activity.

With a buddy, use Skype, Facetime, Twitter or any other communication you have, to play the game "If this is the answer, what is the question?". For example, if you are revising Geography and the answer you provide is "meander", your buddy would have to make up a question like "What is the word that describes a feature of a river where it flows slowly and bends often from side to side?".

Make up 10 "answers" based on the content of the chapter or section you are using. Give this to your buddy to solve while you solve theirs.

Step 4

Construct a wordsearch of at least 10 X 10 squares. You can make it as big as you like but keep it realistic. Work together with a group of friends. Many apps allow you to make wordsearch puzzles online. The words and phrases can go in any direction and phrases can be split. Your puzzle must only contain facts linked to the topic you are revising. Your task is to find 10 bits of information to hide in your puzzle, but you must not repeat information that you used in Step 3. DO NOT show where the words are. Fill up empty squares with random letters. Remember to keep a note of where your answers are hidden but do not show your friends. When you have a complete puzzle, exchange it with a friend to solve each other's puzzle.

Step 5

Now make up 10 questions (not "answers" this time) based on the same chapter used in the previous two tasks. Again, you must find NEW information that you have not yet used. Now it's getting hard to find that new information! Again, give your questions to a friend to answer.

Step 6

As you have been doing the puzzles, your brain has been actively searching for new information. Now write a NEW LIST that contains only the new information you have discovered when doing the puzzles. Your new list is the one to look at repeatedly for short bursts over the next few days. Try to remember more and more of it without looking at it. After a few days, you should be able to add words from your second list to your first list as you increase the information in your long-term memory.

FINALLY! Be inspired...

Make a list of different revision ideas and beside each one write **THINGS I HAVE** tried, **THINGS I WILL** try and **THINGS I MIGHT** try. Don't be scared of trying something new.

And remember – "FAIL TO PREPARE AND PREPARE TO FAIL!"

Intermediate 2 Mathematics Units 1, 2 and 3

The course

Intermediate 2 Mathematics is divided into 3 units. Unit 1 is subdivided into five outcomes (appreciation, volume, straight line, breaking brackets / factorisation and circle work). Unit 2 has four outcomes (trigonometry, simultaneous equations, graphs / charts and statistics). Unit 3 has three outcomes (algebraic topics, quadratic graphs and equations and trigonometric graphs, equations and identities). The Course Arrangements can be accessed and downloaded from the SQA website at www.sqa.org.uk/sqa/39090.html and give more detail on the course content.

Your task is to develop your knowledge of these outcomes and the skills necessary to deal with them and also to demonstrate your understanding by **applying** this knowledge and these skills correctly and appropriately.

How the course is graded

The grade you finally get for Intermediate 2 Mathematics depends on two things:

- the internal assessments you do in school or college (the "NABs") – these don't count towards the final grade, but you must have passed them before you can achieve a final award. It is worth noting here that the "NABs" are set at "minimum competence", i.e. the final examination will be harder and more complex than the "NABs".

- the two exam papers you sit in May – that's what this book is all about!

The exams

Paper 1 lasts for 45 minutes, is worth 30 marks and must be completed without the aid of a calculator.

Paper 2 lasts for 1 hour 30 minutes, is worth 50 marks and a calculator can be used in this paper.

Remember that in both papers there will be a page of formulae that you will find useful. Don't forget to use it!

The papers are designed to contain around 35% of "non-routine" material, i.e. questions where the strategy may not be obvious and you may have to think a bit about how to tackle them. Also 35% of the papers will consist of more difficult questions, e.g. *'Given the volume of a shape, calculate its height'*.

Areas of strength and weakness

In 2012, over 23 000 candidates were presented for Intermediate 2 Mathematics. Across a large number like this it is easy to spot topics which have been done well and also topics where common errors appear.

Where candidates get it right

In general, candidates seem to be more successful in dealing with the material in **Units 1 and 2**. For example, questions on appreciation/depreciation (e.g. 2011, Paper 2 Q2), volume (e.g. 2012, Paper 2 Q3), finding the equation of a straight line (e.g. 2010, Paper 1 Q1), breaking brackets (e.g. 2011, Paper 1 Q2), finding the length of an arc or area of a segment (e.g. 2011, Paper 2 Q5) all seem to be well done, as do basic trigonometric calculations (e.g. 2008, Paper 1 Q6), simultaneous equations (e.g. 2010, Paper 2 Q5), and statistics (e.g. 2010, Paper 1 Q2 or 2009, Paper 2 Q2).

Where candidates have difficulty

Generally, **Unit 3** is found to be more difficult, in particular the algebraic content in Outcome 1 (e.g. 2011, Paper 2 Q9) and trigonometric identities in Outcome 3 (e.g. 2012, Paper 2 Q14). Moreover it is usually taught in the months immediately before the final examination so you might not have the same opportunity to revise and practise this content, although **it is worth noting** that trigonometric identities are usually worth 2 marks, whereas the content in Unit 3 Outcome 1 can be worth 9 or 10 marks.

How to improve your marks

Although material from Units 1 and 2 tends to be tackled more successfully by candidates, when a question is slightly different from those in previous years there can be a disproportionate drop in marks awarded. For example, in 2012, Paper 1 Q3 was a question on the straight line but was different from the normal *"Find the equation of the given line"*. Consequently many candidates did not perform well in this question. You must be prepared to tackle **"non-routine" questions**: they will make up roughly 35% of the total question paper.

No calculator in Paper 1!

Paper 1 has to be tackled without the use of a calculator. In previous years, topics which have been tested in Paper 1 include calculating volume (e.g. 2010, Paper 1 Q3), area of a triangle, using trigonometric formula (e.g. 2012, Paper 1 Q7) and standard deviation (e.g. 2007, Paper 1 Q6). These are all topics which appear more commonly in Paper 2. Because they are in Paper 1, the setters will have chosen the figures carefully so that the calculations do not become too unwieldy. Usually, re-ordering the numbers, or "cancelling" fractions will ease calculations.

Showing working

On the cover of the examination paper, candidates are instructed to **show all working**. This is a very important part of scoring well in the examination. **For all questions worth more than 1 mark, evidence of a method must be shown.** It is especially critical for questions worth 4 or 5 marks. Sometimes for these questions, 4 out of 5 marks are for correct strategies and only 1 mark for correct calculations. So even if you make a mistake in the calculation and arrive at the wrong answer, it may be possible to receive up to 4 out of 5 marks for tackling the problem in an appropriate way. So it is vital that the marker can clearly see the strategy you are following! This would apply in trigonometry questions such as 2010, Paper 2, Q12. Detailed Marking Instructions are available from the SQA website www.sqa.org.uk/sqa/39090.html and these are useful in showing how marks are awarded and what evidence is expected/acceptable.

Communicating strategies

Candidates sometimes find it difficult to **communicate** the strategies being used. They show calculations but, where the question is a complex one, it may be difficult for the marker to see what the numbers in the calculations are referring to. In cases like this it is often very helpful to use a **diagram** to convey information to enable the marker to understand the strategy you are using. In 2012, Paper 1 Q4 (angles in a circle) and Paper 2 Q12 (complex trigonometry problem) were questions in this category. If you are able to mark sizes of lines and angles onto a diagram in your response, you will make it easier for the markers to follow the strategy and to award marks.

Complex trigonometry questions

Complex trigonometry questions are usually worth around 5 marks. Where you see a question like this, try to establish how many triangles are in the diagram and even draw them out separately to enable you to decide on the sizes of sides and angles known in each triangle. Where 5 marks are being awarded for a trigonometry question, it usually means you have to work in 2 different triangles, finding a missing size in one and then using it in a different triangle to find the size asked for in the question.

Statistics questions

Statistics questions are usually very well done. The exception to this is the *interpretation* of statistics, usually tested in part (b) of a question. Generally, candidates will be asked to comment on how two sets of statistics compare, using measures of average (median, mean) and/or measures of spread (semi-interquartile range, standard deviation).

However, it is not enough to say that one standard deviation is greater or smaller than the other. Comparisons must be made **in context** to show some understanding of what the information is telling us. Some candidates have difficulty in explaining the comparisons. In 2012, Paper 2 Q5, candidates performed better than usual, probably because a choice of statements had been given and candidates had simply to pick the appropriate ones. Usually candidates have to devise the form of words in which to express the answer. Again the Detailed Marking Instructions on the SQA website will offer you the various acceptable answers for this type of question.

Be systematic!

A systematic approach is always best. Be sure to download the Arrangements Documents from the SQA website so that you have a checklist for the course content and can be certain you have covered all aspects of the course. Use this book to tackle as many specific topics in past papers as you can! For example, if you want to focus on questions to do with percentage appreciation or depreciation then try all those questions that you can find (there will usually be one per year). If you are stuck on a particular question, get someone to explain how to do it, then **try it by yourself**. Come back to it again at a later date and try it again. Keep a record of the questions you have tried (maybe a tick beside it if you solve it by yourself and a question mark if you have to come back to it again). When you have completed the course then you can try **whole** past papers to check your timing. Older papers are available on the SQA website if you would like a change!

Good luck!

Remember that the rewards for passing Intermediate 2 Mathematics are well worth it! Your pass will help you get the future you want for yourself. In the exam, be confident in your own ability. If you're not sure how to answer a question, trust your instincts and just give it a go anyway – keep calm and don't panic! GOOD LUCK!

INTERMEDIATE 2

2010

[BLANK PAGE]

X100/201

NATIONAL QUALIFICATIONS 2010	FRIDAY, 21 MAY 1.00 PM – 1.45 PM	MATHEMATICS INTERMEDIATE 2 Units 1, 2 and 3 Paper 1 (Non-calculator)

Read carefully

1 **You may <u>NOT</u> use a calculator.**

2 Full credit will be given only where the solution contains appropriate working.

3 Square-ruled paper is provided.

FORMULAE LIST

The roots of $ax^2 + bx + c = 0$ are $x = \dfrac{-b \pm \sqrt{(b^2 - 4ac)}}{2a}$

Sine rule: $\dfrac{a}{\sin A} = \dfrac{b}{\sin B} = \dfrac{c}{\sin C}$

Cosine rule: $a^2 = b^2 + c^2 - 2bc \cos A$ or $\cos A = \dfrac{b^2 + c^2 - a^2}{2bc}$

Area of a triangle: $\text{Area} = \frac{1}{2} ab \sin C$

Volume of a sphere: $\text{Volume} = \frac{4}{3} \pi r^3$

Volume of a cone: $\text{Volume} = \frac{1}{3} \pi r^2 h$

Volume of a cylinder: $\text{Volume} = \pi r^2 h$

Standard deviation: $s = \sqrt{\dfrac{\sum (x - \bar{x})^2}{n-1}} = \sqrt{\dfrac{\sum x^2 - (\sum x)^2 / n}{n-1}}$, where n is the sample size.

Marks

ALL questions should be attempted.

1.

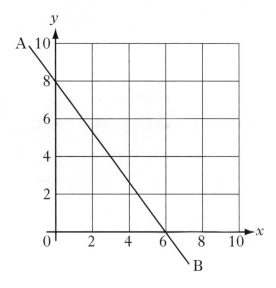

Find the equation of the straight line AB shown in the diagram.   **3**

2. The pupils in a primary class record their shoe sizes as shown below.

8	7	6	5	6
5	7	11	7	7
7	8	7	9	6
8	6	5	9	7

(a) Construct a frequency table from the above data and add a cumulative frequency column.   **2**

(b) For this data, find:

(i) the median;   **1**

(ii) the lower quartile;   **1**

(iii) the upper quartile.   **1**

(c) Construct a boxplot for this data.   **2**

[Turn over

Marks

3. The diagram below represents a sphere.

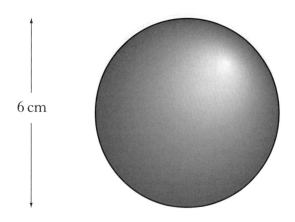

6 cm

The sphere has a diameter of 6 centimetres.

Calculate its volume.

Take $\pi = 3\cdot14$.   2

4. (*a*) Factorise

$$x^2 + x - 6.$$ 2

(*b*) Multiply out the brackets and collect like terms.

$$(3x + 2)(x^2 + 5x - 1)$$ 3

Marks

5. The diagram below shows the graph of $y = -x^2$.

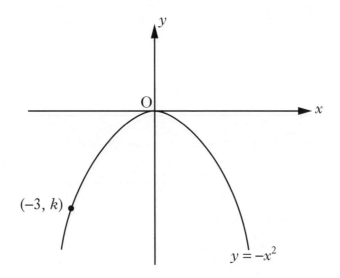

The point $(-3, k)$ lies on the graph.

Find the value of k. 　　　　1

6.

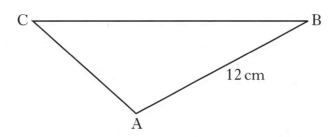

In triangle ABC, AB = 12 centimetres, $\sin C = \frac{1}{2}$ and $\sin B = \frac{1}{3}$.

Find the length of side AC. 　　　　3

[Turn over

Marks

7. Express

$$p^3(p^2 - p^{-3})$$

in its simplest form.   2

8. Maria has been asked to find the roots of the equation

$$x^2 + 3x + 5 = 0.$$

She decides to use the quadratic formula

$$x = \frac{-b \pm \sqrt{(b^2 - 4ac)}}{2a}.$$

(a) Calculate the value of $b^2 - 4ac$.   1

(b) Now explain why Maria cannot find the roots.   1

9. The graph shown below has an equation of the form $y = \cos(x - a)°$.

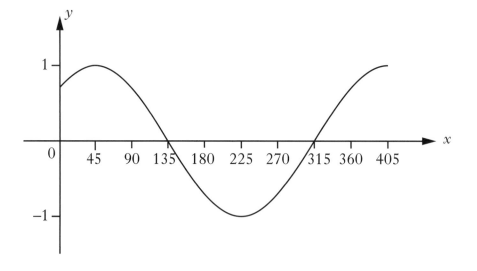

Write down the value of a.   1

Marks

10. The graph below shows part of a parabola with equation of the form $y = (x + a)^2 + b$.

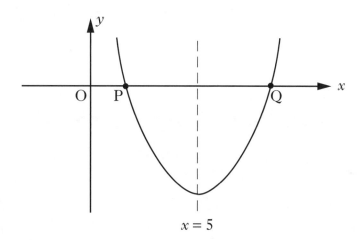

$x = 5$

The equation of the axis of symmetry of the parabola is $x = 5$.

(*a*)   State the value of *a*.   1

(*b*)   P is the point (2, 0). State the coordinates of Q.   1

(*c*)   Calculate the value of *b*.   2

[END OF QUESTION PAPER]

[BLANK PAGE]

X100/203

| NATIONAL QUALIFICATIONS 2010 | FRIDAY, 21 MAY 2.05 PM – 3.35 PM | MATHEMATICS INTERMEDIATE 2 Units 1, 2 and 3 Paper 2 |

Read carefully

1 **Calculators may be used in this paper.**

2 Full credit will be given only where the solution contains appropriate working.

3 Square-ruled paper is provided.

FORMULAE LIST

The roots of $ax^2 + bx + c = 0$ are $x = \dfrac{-b \pm \sqrt{(b^2 - 4ac)}}{2a}$

Sine rule: $\dfrac{a}{\sin A} = \dfrac{b}{\sin B} = \dfrac{c}{\sin C}$

Cosine rule: $a^2 = b^2 + c^2 - 2bc \cos A$ or $\cos A = \dfrac{b^2 + c^2 - a^2}{2bc}$

Area of a triangle: $\text{Area} = \frac{1}{2} ab \sin C$

Volume of a sphere: $\text{Volume} = \frac{4}{3} \pi r^3$

Volume of a cone: $\text{Volume} = \frac{1}{3} \pi r^2 h$

Volume of a cylinder: $\text{Volume} = \pi r^2 h$

Standard deviation: $s = \sqrt{\dfrac{\sum (x - \bar{x})^2}{n - 1}} = \sqrt{\dfrac{\sum x^2 - (\sum x)^2 / n}{n - 1}}$, where n is the sample size.

Marks

ALL questions should be attempted.

1. An industrial machine costs £176 500.

   Its value depreciates by 4·25% each year.

   How much is it worth after 3 years?

   Give your answer correct to **three** significant figures.   4

2. Paul conducts a survey to find the most popular school lunch.

   - 30 pupils vote for Pasta
   - 40 pupils vote for Baked Potato
   - 2 pupils vote for Salad

   Paul wishes to draw a pie chart to illustrate his data. How many degrees must he use for each sector in his pie chart?

   Do not draw the pie chart.   2

3. The scattergraph shows the taxi fare, p pounds, plotted against the distance travelled, m miles. A line of best fit has been drawn.

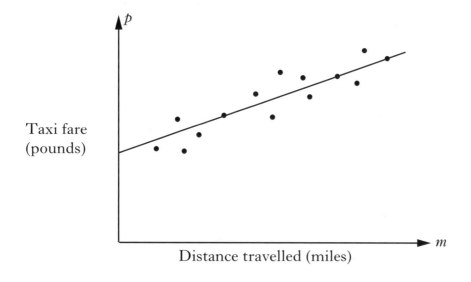

   Taxi fare (pounds)

   Distance travelled (miles)

   The equation of the line of best fit is $p = 2 + 1·5\,m$.

   Use this equation to predict the taxi fare for a journey of 6 miles.   1

   [Turn over

Marks

4. A rugby team scored the following points in a series of matches.

$$13 \quad 7 \quad 0 \quad 9 \quad 7 \quad 8 \quad 5$$

(a) For this sample, calculate:

(i) the mean;   1

(ii) the standard deviation.   3

Show clearly all your working.

The following season, the team appoints a new coach.

A similar series of matches produces a mean of 27 and a standard deviation of 3·25.

(b) Make two valid comparisons about the performance of the team under the new coach.   2

5. Solve algebraically the system of equations

$$2x - 5y = 24$$
$$7x + 8y = 33.$$ 3

6. Express

$$\frac{s^2}{t} \times \frac{3t}{2s}$$

as a fraction in its simplest form.   2

7. Change the subject of the formula

$$P = 2(L + B)$$

to L.   2

Marks

8. Express

$$\sqrt{63} + \sqrt{28} - \sqrt{7}$$

as a surd in its simplest form.

3

9. The ends of a magazine rack are identical.

Each end is a sector of a circle with radius 14 centimetres.
The angle in each sector is 65°.

The sectors are joined by two rectangles, each with length 40 centimetres.

The exterior is covered by material.
What area of material is required?

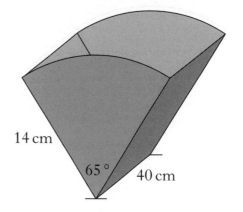

14 cm

65°   40 cm

4

10. The diagram below represents a rectangular garden with length $(x + 7)$ metres and breadth $(x + 3)$ metres.

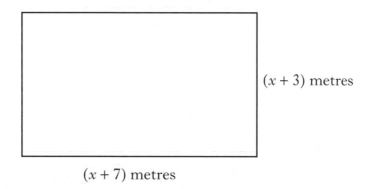

$(x + 3)$ metres

$(x + 7)$ metres

(a) Show that the area, A square metres, of the garden is given by

$$A = x^2 + 10x + 21.$$

2

(b) The area of the garden is 45 square metres. Find x.

Show clearly all your working.

4

Marks

11. A cylindrical container has a volume of 3260 cubic centimetres.

    The radius of the cross section is 6·4 centimetres.

    Calculate the height of the cylinder.

3

12. Two ships have located a wreck on the sea bed.

    In the diagram below, the points P and Q represent the two ships and the point R represents the wreck.

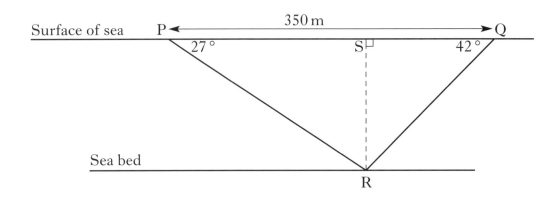

    The angle of depression of R from P is 27°.
    The angle of depression of R from Q is 42°.
    The distance PQ is 350 metres.

    Calculate QS, the distance ship Q has to travel to be directly above the wreck.

    Do not use a scale drawing.

    5

Marks

13. Ocean World has an underwater viewing tunnel.

The diagram below shows the cross-section of the tunnel. It consists of part of a circle with a horizontal base.

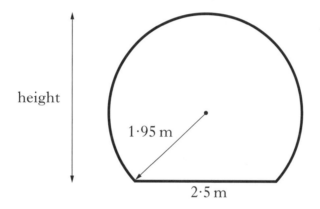

height

1·95 m

2·5 m

The radius of the circle is 1·95 metres and the width of the base is 2·5 metres.

Calculate the height of the tunnel.   4

[Turn over for Question 14 on *Page eight*

Marks

14. A surveyor views a lift as it travels up the outside of a building.

In the diagram below, the point L represents the lift.

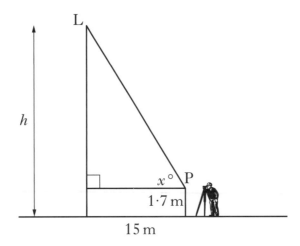

The height, *h* metres, of the lift above the ground is given by the formula

$$h = 15 \tan x° + 1·7,$$

where *x*° is the angle of elevation of the lift from the surveyor at point P.

(*a*) What is the height of the lift above the ground when the angle of elevation from P is 25°?   2

(*b*) What is the angle of elevation at point P when the height of the lift above the ground is 18·4 metres?   3

[END OF QUESTION PAPER]

INTERMEDIATE 2

2011

[BLANK PAGE]

X100/201

NATIONAL QUALIFICATIONS 2011	WEDNESDAY, 18 MAY 1.00 PM – 1.45 PM	MATHEMATICS INTERMEDIATE 2 Units 1, 2 and 3 Paper 1 (Non-calculator)

Read carefully

1 **You may NOT use a calculator.**

2 Full credit will be given only where the solution contains appropriate working.

3 Square-ruled paper is provided. If you make use of this, you should write your name on it clearly and put it inside your answer booklet.

FORMULAE LIST

The roots of $ax^2 + bx + c = 0$ are $x = \dfrac{-b \pm \sqrt{(b^2 - 4ac)}}{2a}$

Sine rule: $\dfrac{a}{\sin A} = \dfrac{b}{\sin B} = \dfrac{c}{\sin C}$

Cosine rule: $a^2 = b^2 + c^2 - 2bc \cos A$ or $\cos A = \dfrac{b^2 + c^2 - a^2}{2bc}$

Area of a triangle: Area $= \frac{1}{2}ab \sin C$

Volume of a sphere: Volume $= \frac{4}{3}\pi r^3$

Volume of a cone: Volume $= \frac{1}{3}\pi r^2 h$

Volume of a cylinder: Volume $= \pi r^2 h$

Standard deviation: $s = \sqrt{\dfrac{\sum(x - \bar{x})^2}{n-1}} = \sqrt{\dfrac{\sum x^2 - (\sum x)^2 / n}{n-1}}$, where n is the sample size.

Marks

ALL questions should be attempted.

1.   Sandi takes the bus to work each day.

Over a two week period, she records the number of minutes the bus is late each day. The results are shown below.

          5   6   15   0   6   11   2   9   8   7

    (*a*)   From the above data, find:

       (i)   the median;   1

       (ii)   the lower quartile;   1

       (iii)   the upper quartile.   1

    (*b*)   Construct a boxplot for the data.   2

Sandi decides to take the train over the next two week period and records the number of minutes the train is late each day.

The boxplot, drawn below, was constructed for the new data.

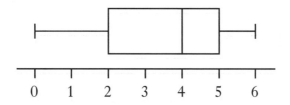

    (*c*)   Compare the two boxplots and comment.   1

2.   Multiply out the brackets and collect like terms.

$$5x + (3x + 2)(2x - 7)$$

                                                           3

[Turn over

Marks

3. A circle, centre O, is shown below.

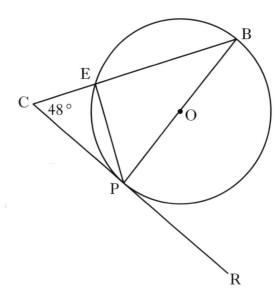

In the circle

- PB is a diameter
- CR is a tangent to the circle at point P
- Angle BCP is 48°.

Calculate the size of angle EPR.   3

4. Three of the following have the same value.

$$2\sqrt{6}, \qquad \sqrt{2} \times \sqrt{12}, \qquad 3\sqrt{8}, \qquad \sqrt{24}.$$

Which one has a different value?

You must give a reason for your answer.   2

Marks

5.

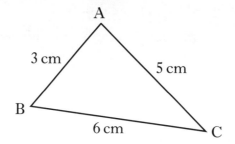

In triangle ABC, show that $\cos B = \dfrac{5}{9}$. **3**

6. Evaluate

$$9^{\frac{3}{2}}.$$

2

7. Part of the graph of $y = a \cos bx^\circ$ is shown in the diagram.

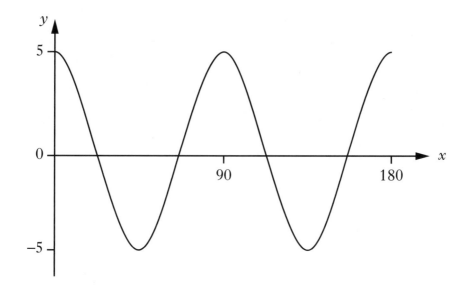

State the values of a and b. **2**

[Turn over

Marks

8. A straight line is represented by the equation $y = mx + c$.

Sketch a possible straight line graph to illustrate this equation when $m > 0$ and $c < 0$.   **2**

9. (*a*) Factorise $x^2 - 4x - 21$.   **2**

(*b*) Hence write down the roots of the equation

$$x^2 - 4x - 21 = 0.$$ **1**

(*c*) The graph of $y = x^2 - 4x - 21$ is shown in the diagram.

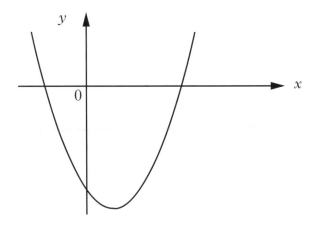

Find the coordinates of the turning point.   **3**

10.

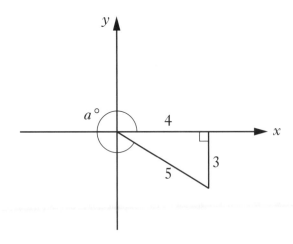

Write down the value of $\cos a°$.   **1**

[END OF QUESTION PAPER]

X100/203

| NATIONAL QUALIFICATIONS 2011 | WEDNESDAY, 18 MAY 2.05 PM – 3.35 PM | MATHEMATICS INTERMEDIATE 2 Units 1, 2 and 3 Paper 2 |

Read carefully

1 **Calculators may be used in this paper.**

2 Full credit will be given only where the solution contains appropriate working.

3 Square-ruled paper is provided. If you make use of this, you should write your name on it clearly and put it inside your answer booklet.

FORMULAE LIST

The roots of $ax^2 + bx + c = 0$ are $x = \dfrac{-b \pm \sqrt{(b^2 - 4ac)}}{2a}$

Sine rule: $\dfrac{a}{\sin A} = \dfrac{b}{\sin B} = \dfrac{c}{\sin C}$

Cosine rule: $a^2 = b^2 + c^2 - 2bc \cos A$ or $\cos A = \dfrac{b^2 + c^2 - a^2}{2bc}$

Area of a triangle: $\text{Area} = \frac{1}{2} ab \sin C$

Volume of a sphere: $\text{Volume} = \frac{4}{3} \pi r^3$

Volume of a cone: $\text{Volume} - \frac{1}{3} \pi r^2 h$

Volume of a cylinder: $\text{Volume} = \pi r^2 h$

Standard deviation: $s = \sqrt{\dfrac{\sum (x - \bar{x})^2}{n - 1}} = \sqrt{\dfrac{\sum x^2 - (\sum x)^2 / n}{n - 1}}$, where n is the sample size.

Marks

ALL questions should be attempted.

1.

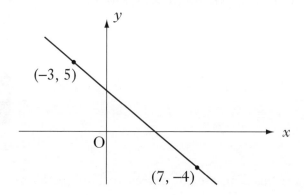

Calculate the gradient of the straight line passing through the points (−3, 5) and (7, −4).

1

2. It is estimated that house prices will increase at the rate of 3·15% per annum.

A house is valued at £134 750. If its value increases at the predicted rate, calculate its value after 3 years.

Give your answer correct to **four** significant figures.

4

3. Change the subject of the formula

$$A = 4\pi r^2$$

to r.

2

[Turn over

Marks

4. The Battle of Largs in 1263 is commemorated by a monument known as The Pencil.

This monument is in the shape of a cylinder with a cone on top.

The cylinder part has diameter 3 metres and height 15 metres.

(*a*) Calculate the volume of the **cylinder** part of The Pencil.   **2**

The volume of the **cone** part of The Pencil is 5·7 cubic metres.

(*b*) Calculate the **total** height of The Pencil.   **3**

5. The diagram below shows a sector of a circle, centre C.

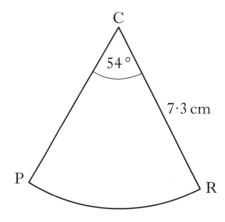

The radius of the circle is 7·3 centimetres and angle PCR is 54°.

Calculate the area of the sector PCR.   **3**

Marks

6. A sample of six boxes contains the following numbers of pins per box.

   43   39   41   40   39   44

   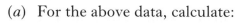

   (a) For the above data, calculate:

   (i) the mean;   1

   (ii) the standard deviation.   3

   The company which produces the pins claims that "the mean number of pins per box is 40 ± 2 and the standard deviation is less than 3".

   (b) Does the data in part (a) support the claim made by the company?

   Give reasons for your answer.   2

7. Alan is taking part in a quiz. He is awarded x points for each correct answer and y points for each wrong answer. During the quiz, Alan gets 24 questions correct and 6 wrong. He scores 60 points.

   (a) Write down an equation in x and y which satisfies the above condition.   1

   Helen also takes part in the quiz. She gets 20 questions correct and 10 wrong. She scores 40 points.

   (b) Write down a second equation in x and y which satisfies this condition.   1

   (c) Calculate the score for David who gets 17 correct and 13 wrong.   4

8. Simplify

   $$\frac{3x-15}{(x-5)^2}.$$ 2

9. Express

   $$\frac{3}{x} - \frac{4}{x+1}, \qquad x \neq 0, \ x \neq -1$$

   as a single fraction in its simplest form.   3

Marks

10. Solve the equation

$$2 \tan x° - 3 = 5, \qquad 0 \le x \le 360.$$

3

11. Solve the equation

$$4x^2 - 7x + 1 = 0,$$

giving the roots correct to 1 decimal place.

4

12.

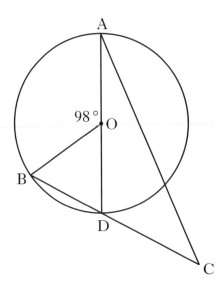

AD is a diameter of a circle, centre O.
B is a point on the circumference of the circle.
The chord BD is extended to a point C, outside the circle.
Angle BOA = 98°.
DC = 9 centimetres. The radius of the circle is 7 centimetres.

Calculate the length of AC.

5

Marks

13. A circular saw can be adjusted to change the depth of blade that is exposed below the horizontal guide.

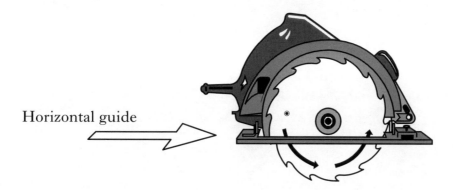

Horizontal guide

The circle, centre O, below represents the blade and the line AB represents part of the horizontal guide.

This blade has a radius of 110 millimetres.

If AB has length 140 millimetres, calculate the depth, *d* millimetres, of saw exposed.

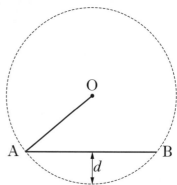

4

14. Prove that

$$\frac{\sin^2 A}{1 - \sin^2 A} = \tan^2 A.$$

2

[*END OF QUESTION PAPER*]

[BLANK PAGE]

INTERMEDIATE 2

2012

[BLANK PAGE]

X100/11/01

NATIONAL
QUALIFICATIONS
2012

MONDAY, 21 MAY
9.00 AM – 9.45 AM

MATHEMATICS
INTERMEDIATE 2
Units 1, 2 and 3
Paper 1
(Non-calculator)

Read carefully

1   **You may NOT use a calculator.**

2   Full credit will be given only where the solution contains appropriate working.

3   Square-ruled paper is provided. If you make use of this, you should write your name on it clearly and put it inside your answer booklet.

FORMULAE LIST

The roots of $ax^2 + bx + c = 0$ are $x = \dfrac{-b \pm \sqrt{(b^2 - 4ac)}}{2a}$

Sine rule: $\dfrac{a}{\sin A} = \dfrac{b}{\sin B} = \dfrac{c}{\sin C}$

Cosine rule: $a^2 = b^2 + c^2 - 2bc \cos A$ or $\cos A = \dfrac{b^2 + c^2 - a^2}{2bc}$

Area of a triangle: Area $= \frac{1}{2} ab \sin C$

Volume of a sphere: Volume $= \frac{4}{3} \pi r^3$

Volume of a cone: Volume $= \frac{1}{3} \pi r^2 h$

Volume of a cylinder: Volume $= \pi r^2 h$

Standard deviation: $s = \sqrt{\dfrac{\sum (x - \bar{x})^2}{n-1}} = \sqrt{\dfrac{\sum x^2 - (\sum x)^2 / n}{n-1}}$, where n is the sample size.

ALL questions should be attempted.   *Marks*

1. The National Debt of the United Kingdom was recently calculated as

    £1 157 818 887 139.

    Round this amount to four significant figures.   1

2. A teacher recorded the marks, out of ten, of a group of pupils for a spelling test.

Mark	Frequency
5	2
6	5
7	6
8	11
9	9
10	2

    (a) Copy the frequency table and add a cumulative frequency column.   1

    (b) For this data, find:

        (i)   the median;   1

        (ii) the lower quartile;   1

        (iii) the upper quartile.   1

    (c) Draw a boxplot to illustrate this data.   2

[Turn over

Marks

3. The straight line with equation $4x + 3y = 36$ cuts the y-axis at A.

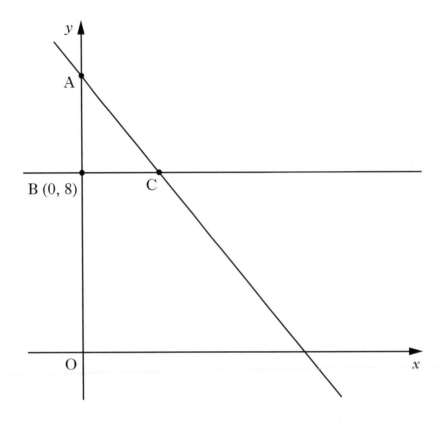

(*a*) Find the coordinates of A.   1

This line meets the line through B (0, 8), parallel to the x-axis, at C as shown above.

(*b*) Find the coordinates of C.   2

Marks

4.

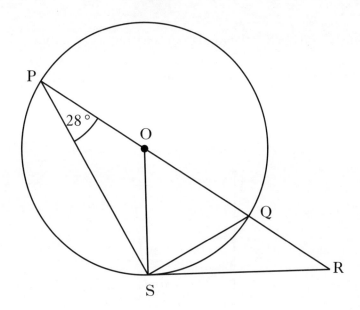

In the above diagram,

- O is the centre of the circle
- PQ is a diameter of the circle
- PQR is a straight line
- RS is a tangent to the circle at S
- angle OPS is 28°.

Calculate the size of angle QRS.   **3**

5. One weekend, the attendances at five Premier League football matches were recorded.

8 900	12 700	59 200	10 300	9 700

The median attendance is 10 300.

(*a*) Calculate the mean attendance.   **1**

(*b*) Which of the two "averages" – the mean or the median – is more representative of the data?

You must explain your answer.   **1**

[Turn over

Marks

6. The equation $x^2 - 6x + 8 = 0$ can also be written as $(x - 2)(x - 4) = 0$.

   (a) Write down the roots of the equation $x^2 - 6x + 8 = 0$.   **1**

   Part of the graph of $y = x^2 - 6x + 8$ is shown below.

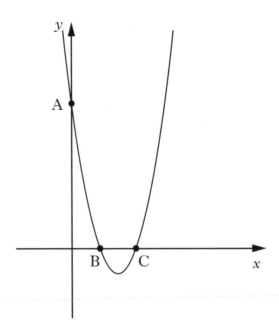

   (b) State the coordinates of the points A, B and C.   **3**

   (c) What is the equation of the axis of symmetry of this graph?   **1**

Marks

7.

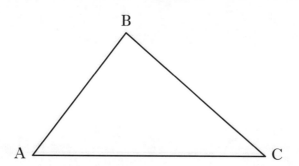

The area of triangle ABC is 20 square centimetres.

AC = 16 centimetres and $\sin C = \frac{1}{4}$.

Calculate the length of BC.

2

8. (*a*) Factorise

$$a^2 + 2ab + b^2.$$

1

(*b*) Hence, or otherwise, find the value of

$$94^2 + 2 \times 94 \times 6 + 6^2.$$

2

9. Sketch the graph of $y = -2 \sin x°$, $0 \le x \le 360$.

3

10. Simplify $\sqrt{2}\left(\sqrt{3} + \sqrt{2}\right) - \sqrt{6}$.

2

[END OF QUESTION PAPER]

[BLANK PAGE]

X100/11/02

NATIONAL
QUALIFICATIONS
2012

MONDAY, 21 MAY
10.05 AM – 11.35 AM

MATHEMATICS
INTERMEDIATE 2
Units 1, 2 and 3
Paper 2

Read carefully

1 **Calculators may be used in this paper.**

2 Full credit will be given only where the solution contains appropriate working.

3 Square-ruled paper is provided. If you make use of this, you should write your name on it clearly and put it inside your answer booklet.

FORMULAE LIST

The roots of $ax^2 + bx + c = 0$ are $x = \dfrac{-b \pm \sqrt{(b^2 - 4ac)}}{2a}$

Sine rule: $\dfrac{a}{\sin A} = \dfrac{b}{\sin B} = \dfrac{c}{\sin C}$

Cosine rule: $a^2 = b^2 + c^2 - 2bc \cos A$ or $\cos A = \dfrac{b^2 + c^2 - a^2}{2bc}$

Area of a triangle: $\text{Area} = \frac{1}{2}ab \sin C$

Volume of a sphere: $\text{Volume} = \frac{4}{3}\pi r^3$

Volume of a cone: $\text{Volume} = \frac{1}{3}\pi r^2 h$

Volume of a cylinder: $\text{Volume} = \pi r^2 h$

Standard deviation: $s = \sqrt{\dfrac{\sum(x - \bar{x})^2}{n-1}} = \sqrt{\dfrac{\sum x^2 - (\sum x)^2 / n}{n-1}}$, where n is the sample size.

ALL questions should be attempted.   *Marks*

1. The diagram below shows a circle, centre C.

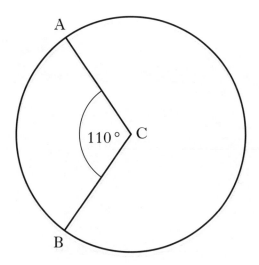

The circumference of the circle is 40·8 centimetres.

Calculate the length of the minor arc AB.   2

2. Multiply out the brackets and collect like terms.

$$(3x - 5)(x^2 + 2x - 6)$$ 3

[Turn over

Marks

3. A health food shop produces cod liver oil capsules for its customers.

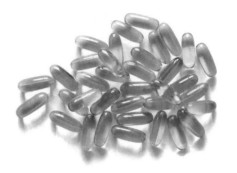

Each capsule is in the shape of a cylinder with hemispherical ends as shown in the diagram below.

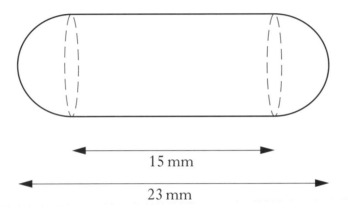

15 mm

23 mm

The total length of the capsule is 23 millimetres and the length of the cylinder is 15 millimetres.

Calculate the volume of one cod liver oil capsule.

4

4. Solve the equation

   $$3x^2 + 7x - 5 = 0,$$

   giving the roots correct to one decimal place.

   Marks

   4

5. A ten-pin bowling team recorded the following six scores in a match.

   | 134 | 102 | 127 | 98 | 104 | 131 |

   (a) For this sample calculate:

   (i) the mean;

   (ii) the standard deviation.

   Show clearly all your working.

   4

   In their second match their six scores have a mean of 116 and a standard deviation of 12·2.

   (b) Consider the 5 statements written below.

   1 The total of the scores is the same in both matches.

   2 The total of the scores is greater in the first match.

   3 The total of the scores is greater in the second match.

   4 In the first match the scores are more spread out.

   5 In the second match the scores are more spread out.

   Which of these statements is/are true?

   2

6. Three groups are booking a holiday. The first group consists of 6 adults and 2 children. The total cost of their holiday is £3148.

   Let x pounds be the cost for an adult and y pounds be the cost for a child.

   (a) Write down an equation in x and y which satisfies the above information.

   1

   The second group books the same holiday for 5 adults and 3 children. The total cost of their holiday is £3022.

   (b) Write down a second equation in x and y which satisfies this information.

   1

   (c) The third group books the same holiday for 2 adults and 4 children. The travel agent calculates that the total cost is £2056.

   Has this group been overcharged?

   Justify your answer.

   4

Marks

7. Express as a single fraction

$$\frac{a}{b} + \frac{b}{a}, \quad a \neq 0, \quad b \neq 0.$$

2

8. Solve the equation $5 \cos x^\circ - 3 = 1$, $0 \leq x \leq 360$.

3

9. A formula used to calculate lighting efficiency is

$$E = \frac{I}{D^2}.$$

Change the subject of this formula to D.

3

10. A tanker delivers oil to garages.

The tank has a circular cross-section as shown in the diagram below.

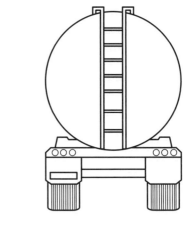

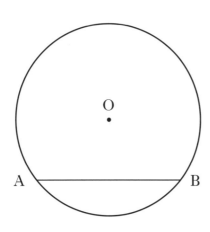

Depth of oil

The radius of the circle, centre O, is 1·9 metres.

The width of the surface of the oil, represented by AB in the diagram, is 2·2 metres.

Calculate the depth of the oil in the tanker.

4

Marks

11. Simplify, expressing your answer with positive indices.

$$(x^2 y^4) \div (x^{-3} y^6)$$

2

12. A yacht and a canoe can be seen from a clifftop.

In the diagram below, Y and C represent the positions of the yacht and the canoe.

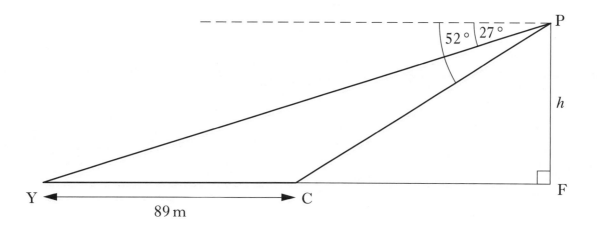

From a point P on the clifftop:

- the angle of depression of the yacht is 27°;
- the angle of depression of the canoe is 52°.

The distance between the yacht and the canoe is 89 metres.

Calculate the height, h, metres, of the cliff.

5

[Turn over

Marks

13. Due to the threat of global warming, scientists recommended in 2010 that the emissions of greenhouse gases should be reduced by 50% by the year 2050.

The government decided to reduce the emissions of greenhouse gases by 15% **every ten years**, starting in the year 2010.

Will the scientists' recommendations have been achieved by 2050?

You must give a reason for your answer.

4

14. Simplify $\dfrac{\cos x^\circ \, \tan x^\circ}{\sin x^\circ}$.

2

[END OF QUESTION PAPER]

INTERMEDIATE 2

2013

[BLANK PAGE]

X100/11/01

| NATIONAL QUALIFICATIONS 2013 | WEDNESDAY, 22 MAY 9.00 AM – 9.45 AM | MATHEMATICS INTERMEDIATE 2 Units 1, 2 and 3 Paper 1 (Non-calculator) |

Read carefully

1 **You may NOT use a calculator.**

2 Full credit will be given only where the solution contains appropriate working.

3 Square-ruled paper is provided. If you make use of this, you should write your name on it clearly and put it inside your answer booklet.

FORMULAE LIST

The roots of $ax^2 + bx + c = 0$ are $x = \dfrac{-b \pm \sqrt{(b^2 - 4ac)}}{2a}$

Sine rule: $\qquad \dfrac{a}{\sin A} = \dfrac{b}{\sin B} = \dfrac{c}{\sin C}$

Cosine rule: $\quad a^2 = b^2 + c^2 - 2bc \cos A \ $ or $ \ \cos A = \dfrac{b^2 + c^2 - a^2}{2bc}$

Area of a triangle: $\qquad$ Area $= \frac{1}{2} ab \sin C$

Volume of a sphere: $\qquad$ Volume $= \frac{4}{3} \pi r^3$

Volume of a cone: $\qquad$ Volume $= \frac{1}{3} \pi r^2 h$

Volume of a cylinder: $\qquad$ Volume $= \pi r^2 h$

Standard deviation: $\qquad s = \sqrt{\dfrac{\sum (x - \bar{x})^2}{n-1}} = \sqrt{\dfrac{\sum x^2 - (\sum x)^2 / n}{n-1}}$, where n is the sample size.

ALL questions should be attempted.   *Marks*

1. Factorise

$$6ab - 7bc.$$ 1

2.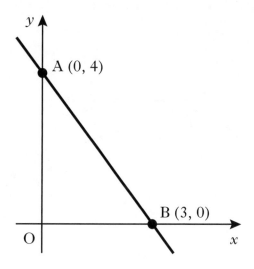

Find the equation of the straight line AB.   3

3. The diagram below shows a sector of a circle, centre C.

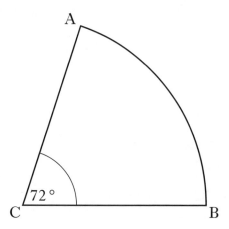

The radius of the circle is 5 centimetres and angle ACB is $72\,^{\circ}$.

Calculate the length of arc AB.

Take π = 3·14.   3

[Turn over

Marks

4. Solve algebraically the system of equations

$$2x - y = 10$$
$$4x + 5y = 6.$$

3

5.

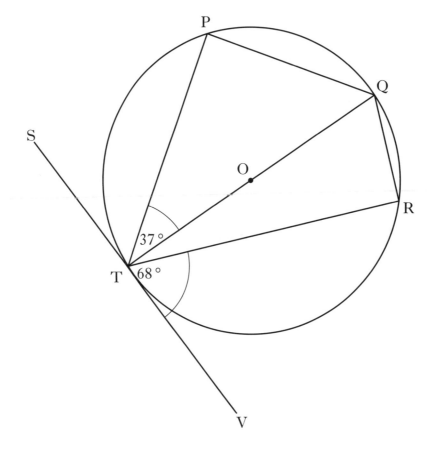

The tangent SV touches the circle, centre O, at T.

Angle PTQ is 37° and angle VTR is 68°.

Calculate the size of angle PQR.

3

Marks

6. The stem and leaf diagram shows the number of minutes on average spent on homework per night by a group of first year pupils.

$$
\begin{array}{r|llllllllll}
1 & 0 & 5 & 5 & 5 \\
2 & 0 & 1 & 2 & 2 & 3 & 5 & 5 & 8 & 9 \\
3 & 0 & 5 & 5 & 6 & 6 & 7 & 8 & 9 & 9 & 9 \\
4 & 2 & 4 & 4 & 5 & 6 & 7 \\
5 & 0 \\
\end{array}
$$

n = 30   1 | 0 represents 10 minutes

(a) Using the above data find:

   (i) the median;   1

   (ii) the lower quartile;   1

   (iii) the upper quartile.   1

(b) Draw a boxplot to illustrate this data.   2

(c) A group of fourth year pupils was surveyed to find out how many minutes on average they spent on homework per night. The boxplot below was drawn for this data.

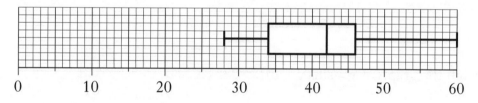

Compare the two boxplots and comment.   2

7. Simplify $\dfrac{(x+4)^2}{x^2 - x - 20}$.   3

8. State the period of $y = \sin 2x\,°$.   1

[Turn over

Marks

9. The diagram below shows part of the graph of $y = 20 - (x - 4)^2$.

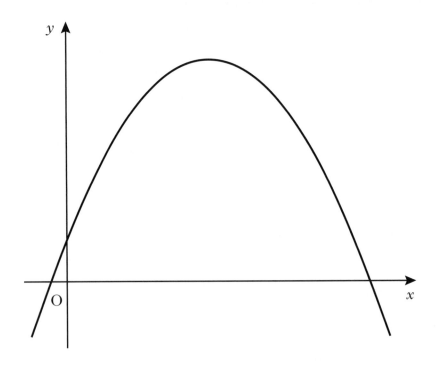

    (*a*) State the coordinates of the maximum turning point.   2

    (*b*) State the equation of the axis of symmetry.   1

10. Sketch the graph of $y = \sin(x - 90)°, \ 0 \le x \le 360$.   3

[END OF QUESTION PAPER]

X100/11/02

| NATIONAL QUALIFICATIONS 2013 | WEDNESDAY, 22 MAY 10.05 AM – 11.35 AM | MATHEMATICS INTERMEDIATE 2 Units 1, 2 and 3 Paper 2 |

Read carefully

1 **Calculators may be used in this paper.**

2 Full credit will be given only where the solution contains appropriate working.

3 Square-ruled paper is provided. If you make use of this, you should write your name on it clearly and put it inside your answer booklet.

FORMULAE LIST

The roots of $ax^2 + bx + c = 0$ are $x = \dfrac{-b \pm \sqrt{(b^2 - 4ac)}}{2a}$

Sine rule: $\dfrac{a}{\sin A} = \dfrac{b}{\sin B} = \dfrac{c}{\sin C}$

Cosine rule: $a^2 = b^2 + c^2 - 2bc \cos A$ or $\cos A = \dfrac{b^2 + c^2 - a^2}{2bc}$

Area of a triangle: $\text{Area} = \frac{1}{2}ab \sin C$

Volume of a sphere: $\text{Volume} = \frac{4}{3}\pi r^3$

Volume of a cone: $\text{Volume} = \frac{1}{3}\pi r^2 h$

Volume of a cylinder: $\text{Volume} = \pi r^2 h$

Standard deviation: $s = \sqrt{\dfrac{\sum(x - \bar{x})^2}{n - 1}} = \sqrt{\dfrac{\sum x^2 - (\sum x)^2 / n}{n - 1}}$, where n is the sample size.

ALL questions should be attempted.

Marks

1. Multiply out the brackets and collect like terms.

   $$(x + 2)(x - 5) - 9x$$

   3

2. A company buys machinery worth £750 000.

   The value of the machinery depreciates by 20% per annum.

   The machinery will be replaced at the end of the year in which its value falls below half of its original value.

   After how many years should the machinery be replaced?

   You must explain your answer.

   4

3. A sample of voters was asked how they intended to vote at the next election. The responses are shown below.

Party	Percentage
Scottish National Party (SNP)	35%
Labour (Lab)	30%
Liberal Democrat (Lib Dem)	15%
Conservative (Con)	10%
Others	10%

   Construct a pie chart to illustrate this information.

   Show all of your working.

   3

   [Turn over

Marks

4. Triangle PQR is shown below.

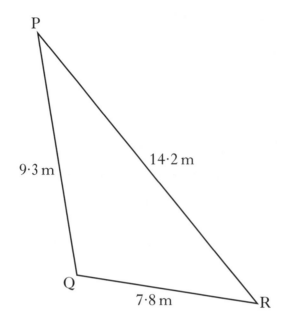

Calculate the size of angle QPR.   3

5. Solve the equation

$$x^2 - 5x - 2 = 0,$$

giving the roots correct to one decimal place.   4

Marks

6. Harry often plays golf and the scores for some of his games are recorded below.

84   78   87   80   81

    (*a*) For this sample calculate:

        (i) the mean;   **1**

        (ii) the standard deviation.   **3**

    Show clearly all your working.

    (*b*) His partner for these games is Tony, whose scores are listed below.

104   98   107   100   101

    Write down the mean and standard deviation of Tony's scores.   **2**

7. A lead **cube**, of side 10 centimetres, is melted down.

During this process 8% of the metal is lost.

The remaining metal is then made into a **cone**, with radius 8 centimetres.

Calculate the height of this cone.

Give your answer correct to 2 significant figures.   **5**

8. Change the subject of the formula

$$a = 3b^2 + c$$

to *b*.   **3**

9. Simplify $\dfrac{x^6}{y^2} \times \dfrac{y^3}{x^3}$.   **2**

[Turn over

Marks

10. A tree surgeon is asked to reduce the height of a tree.

In the diagram below TB represents the original height of the tree and C is the point where the cut is to be made.

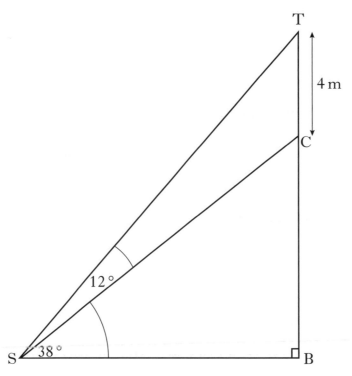

The tree surgeon will reduce the height of the tree by 4 metres.

Angle TSC = 12° and angle BSC = 38°.

Calculate the height of the tree after it has been cut.

Do not use a scale drawing.   5

11. Express

$$\frac{3}{x+2}+\frac{5}{x-1} \qquad x \neq -2, \quad x \neq 1$$

as a single fraction in its simplest form.   3

Marks

12. The shape below is used as a logo in an advertising campaign. It is made up from segments of two identical circles.

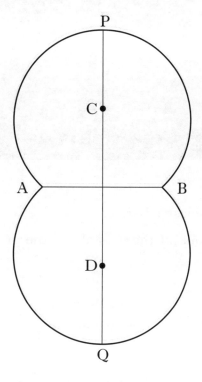

The points C and D are the centres of the circles and each circle has a radius of 24 centimetres.

AB is a common chord of length 30 centimetres.

Calculate the height of the logo, represented by the line PQ.   **5**

[Turn over for Question 13 on *Page eight*

Marks

13.

A Ferris wheel is turning at a steady rate.

The height, h metres, of one of the cars above the ground at a time t seconds is given by the formula

$$h = 7 + 5\sin t°.$$

Find **two** times during the first turn when the car is at a height of 10·8 metres above the ground.

4

[END OF QUESTION PAPER]

Acknowledgements

Permission has been sought from all relevant copyright holders and Hodder Gibson is grateful for the use of the following:
Image © Vitalliy/Shutterstock.com (2013, Paper 2, page 8).

[BLANK PAGE]

X100/11/01

NATIONAL QUALIFICATIONS 2014	TUESDAY, 6 MAY 9.00 AM – 9.45 AM	MATHEMATICS INTERMEDIATE 2 Units 1, 2 and 3 Paper 1 (Non-calculator)

Read carefully

1 **You may NOT use a calculator.**

2 Full credit will be given only where the solution contains appropriate working.

3 Square-ruled paper is provided. If you make use of this, you should write your name on it clearly and put it inside your answer booklet.

FORMULAE LIST

The roots of $ax^2 + bx + c = 0$ are $x = \dfrac{-b \pm \sqrt{(b^2 - 4ac)}}{2a}$

Sine rule: $\dfrac{a}{\sin A} = \dfrac{b}{\sin B} = \dfrac{c}{\sin C}$

Cosine rule: $a^2 = b^2 + c^2 - 2bc \cos A$ or $\cos A = \dfrac{b^2 + c^2 - a^2}{2bc}$

Area of a triangle: $\text{Area} = \frac{1}{2}ab \sin C$

Volume of a sphere: $\text{Volume} = \frac{4}{3}\pi r^3$

Volume of a cone: $\text{Volume} = \frac{1}{3}\pi r^2 h$

Volume of a cylinder: $\text{Volume} = \pi r^2 h$

Standard deviation: $s = \sqrt{\dfrac{\Sigma(x - \bar{x})^2}{n-1}} = \sqrt{\dfrac{\Sigma x^2 - (\Sigma x)^2 / n}{n-1}}$, where n is the sample size.

ALL questions should be attempted.

Marks

1.

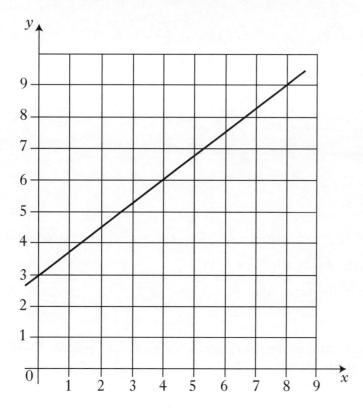

Find the equation of the straight line shown in the diagram above.

3

2. Multiply out the brackets and collect like terms.

$$(3x + 2)(x - 5) + 8x$$

3

[Turn over

Marks

3.

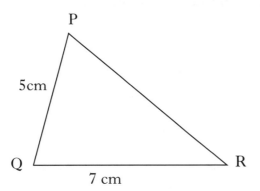

In triangle PQR, PQ = 5 centimetres, QR = 7 centimetres and $\cos Q = \dfrac{1}{5}$.

Calculate the length of side PR.

Give your answer in the form $\sqrt{a}$.   **3**

4. At a ski resort the temperature, in degrees Celsius, was recorded each day at noon for the first fortnight in February 2013.

0 −1 2 −5 4 2 −3 1 −4 8 −6 4 −2 1

(*a*) Calculate:

    (i) the median temperature;   **1**

    (ii) the lower quartile;   **1**

    (iii) the upper quartile.   **1**

(*b*) Use the above data to construct a boxplot.   **2**

(*c*) The temperature, in degrees Celsius, was recorded at the same ski resort each day at noon for the first fortnight in February 2014.

The following boxplot was constructed.

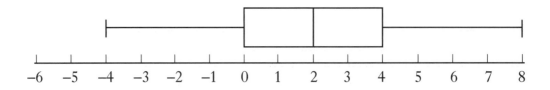

Compare the two boxplots and comment.   **2**

Marks

5. Express $\sqrt{40} + 4\sqrt{10} + \sqrt{90}$ as a surd in its simplest form.

3

6. The diagram below shows part of the graph of $y = ax^2$.

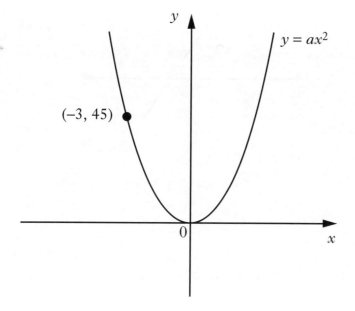

Find the value of a.

2

[Turn over

Marks

7.

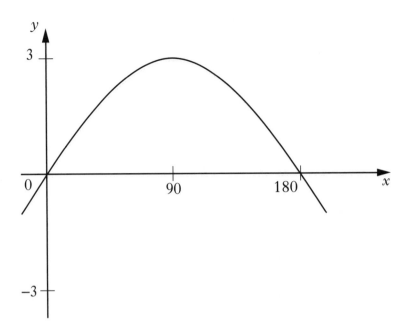

Part of the graph of $y = a \sin bx°$ is shown in the diagram.

State the values of a and b. **2**

8. A parabola has equation $y = (x - 2)^2 - 5$.

(*a*) Write down the coordinates of the turning point of the parabola. **2**

(*b*) Does this parabola have a maximum or a minimum turning point? **1**

Marks

9. The diagram below shows a circle, centre C.

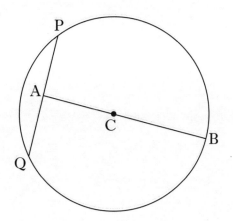

The radius of the circle is 15 centimetres.

A is the mid-point of chord PQ.

The length of AB is 27 centimetres.

Calculate the length of PQ.   **4**

[END OF QUESTION PAPER]

[BLANK PAGE]

X100/11/02

NATIONAL QUALIFICATIONS 2014	TUESDAY, 6 MAY 10.05 AM – 11.35 AM	MATHEMATICS INTERMEDIATE 2 Units 1, 2 and 3 Paper 2

Read carefully

1 **Calculators may be used in this paper.**

2 Full credit will be given only where the solution contains appropriate working.

3 Square-ruled paper is provided. If you make use of this, you should write your name on it clearly and put it inside your answer booklet.

FORMULAE LIST

The roots of $ax^2 + bx + c = 0$ are $x = \dfrac{-b \pm \sqrt{(b^2 - 4ac)}}{2a}$

Sine rule: $\dfrac{a}{\sin A} = \dfrac{b}{\sin B} = \dfrac{c}{\sin C}$

Cosine rule: $a^2 = b^2 + c^2 - 2bc \cos A$ or $\cos A = \dfrac{b^2 + c^2 - a^2}{2bc}$

Area of a triangle: $\text{Area} = \frac{1}{2}ab \sin C$

Volume of a sphere: $\text{Volume} = \frac{4}{3}\pi r^3$

Volume of a cone: $\text{Volume} = \frac{1}{3}\pi r^2 h$

Volume of a cylinder: $\text{Volume} = \pi r^2 h$

Standard deviation: $s = \sqrt{\dfrac{\Sigma (x - \bar{x})^2}{n - 1}} = \sqrt{\dfrac{\Sigma x^2 - (\Sigma x)^2 / n}{n - 1}}$, where n is the sample size.

ALL questions should be attempted.   *Marks*

1. There are 964 pupils on the roll of Aberleven High School.

   It is forecast that the roll will decrease by 15% per year.

   What will be the expected roll after 3 years?

   Give your answer to the nearest ten.   **3**

2. (*a*) A candle is in the shape of a cylinder with diameter 10 centimetres and height 15 centimetres.

   Calculate the volume of the candle.

   Give your answer correct to 3 significant figures.   **3**

   (*b*) A second candle is in the shape of a cone with a circular base of diameter 14 centimetres and height *h* centimetres.

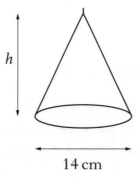

14 cm

   It has the same volume as the first candle.

   Calculate *h*.   **3**

   [Turn over

Marks

3. Factorise **fully**

$$3x^2 + 9x - 12.$$

3

4. Mr Smith and Mrs Curran both shop at the same store.

(a) Mr Smith bought 3 loaves and 2 packets of butter. The total cost was £4·73.

Let x pounds be the cost of a loaf and y pounds be the cost of a packet of butter.

Write down an equation in x and y which satisfies the above condition.

1

(b) Mrs Curran bought 5 loaves and 3 packets of butter. The total cost was £7·52.

Write down a second equation in x and y which satisfies this condition.

1

(c) Use the equations in parts (a) and (b) to find the cost of a loaf and the cost of a packet of butter.

4

5. A runner has recorded her times, in seconds, for six different laps of the running track.

53   57   58   60   55   56

(a) Calculate:

(i) the mean;

1

(ii) the standard deviation;

3

of these lap times.

Show clearly all your working.

(b) She changes her training routine hoping to improve her consistency. After this change, she records her times for another six laps.

The mean is 55 seconds and the standard deviation 3·2 seconds.

Has the new training routine improved her consistency?

Explain clearly your answer.

1

Marks

6. Solve the equation

$$2x^2 - 7x + 1 = 0,$$

giving the answers correct to two decimal places.   **4**

7. Change the subject of the formula

$$p = \frac{qr^2}{3} \quad \text{to } r.$$ **3**

8. Simplify $\dfrac{8p^6}{2p^3 \times p}$.   **3**

9. Express

$$\frac{2}{(x-4)} + \frac{5}{x}, \qquad x \neq 0, \ x \neq 4,$$

as a single fraction in its simplest form.   **3**

[Turn over

Marks

10. Gerry saves 2 pence, 5 pence and 10 pence coins in a jar.

   He thinks the probability of picking a 5 pence coin at random from the jar is $\frac{25}{20}$.

   Why is he wrong?   1

11. In a race, boats sail round three buoys represented by A, B and C in the diagram below.

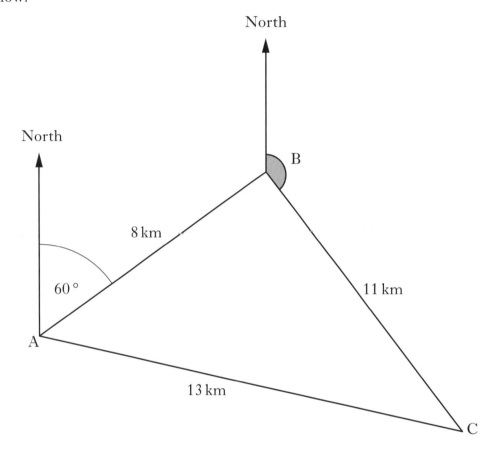

   B is 8 kilometres from A on a bearing of 060°.

   C is 11 kilometres from B.

   A is 13 kilometres from C.

   (*a*) Calculate the size of angle ABC.   3

   (*b*) Hence find the size of the shaded angle.   2

Marks

12.   The barrier at a level crossing is raised after a train has passed.

The height, *h* centimetres, of the end of the barrier can be calculated using the formula below

$$h = 320 \sin x° + 150, \quad 0 \le x \le 90,$$

where $x°$ is the size of the angle between the barrier and the horizontal.

Calculate the size of the angle between the barrier and the horizontal when the height of the end of the barrier is 458 centimetres.   **3**

[Turn over for Question 13 on *Page eight*

Marks

13. The picture shows the entrance to a tunnel which is in the shape of part of a circle.

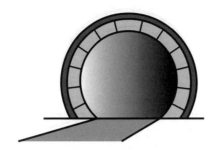

The diagram below represents the cross-section of the tunnel.

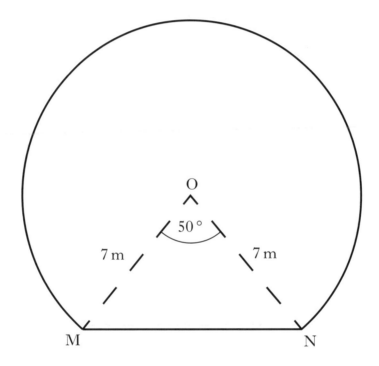

- The centre of the circle is O.
- MN is a chord of the circle.
- Angle MON is 50°.
- The radius of the circle is 7 metres.

Calculate the area of the cross-section of the tunnel.

5

[END OF QUESTION PAPER]

INTERMEDIATE 2 | ANSWER SECTION

MATHEMATICS INTERMEDIATE 2 UNITS 1, 2 AND 3 PAPER 1 (NON-CALCULATOR) 2010

1. $y = -\frac{4}{3}x + 8$

2. (*a*)

Shoe size	frequency	cumulative frequency
5	3	3
6	4	7
7	7	14
8	3	17
9	2	19
10	0	19
11	1	20

   (*b*) (i) 7   (ii) 6   (iii) 8

   (*c*)

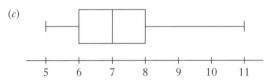

3. 113·04 cubic centimetres

4. (*a*) $(x + 3)(x - 2)$

   (*b*) $3x^3 + 17x^2 + 7x - 2$

5. -9

6. 8 centimetres

7. $p^5 - 1$

8. (*a*) -11

   (*b*) The square root of a negative number does not exist

9. 45

10. (*a*) -5

    (*b*) $(8, 0)$

    (*c*) -9

MATHEMATICS INTERMEDIATE 2 UNITS 1, 2 AND 3 PAPER 2 2010

1. £155 000

2. 150°, 200°, 10°

3. £11

4. (*a*) (i) 7   (ii) 3·958

   (*b*) The team scores more points under the new coach. The team is more consistent.

5. $x = 7, y = -2$

6. $\frac{3s}{2}$

7. $L = \frac{P}{2} - B$ or $L = \frac{P - 2B}{2}$

8. $4\sqrt{7}$

9. 1342·35 square centimetres

10. (*a*) Proof
    $(x + 7)(x + 3)$
    evidence of four correct terms
    $x^2 + 7x + 3x + 21$ leading to
    $x^2 + 10x + 21$

    (*b*) $x = 2$

11. 25·3 centimetres

12. 126·5 metres

13. 3·45 metres

14. (*a*) 8·69 metres

    (*b*) 48°

MATHEMATICS INTERMEDIATE 2 UNITS 1, 2 AND 3 PAPER 1 (NON-CALCULATOR) 2011

1. (a) (i) $Q_2 = 6.5$
   (ii) $Q_1 = 5$
   (iii) $Q_3 = 9$

   (b)

   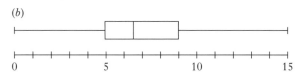

   (c) The trains are not as late as the buses
   or the trains are more reliable

2. $6x^2 - 12x - 14$

3. $138°$

4. $3\sqrt{8}$ with evidence

5. To prove $\cos B = \dfrac{5}{9}$

   $$\cos B = \frac{a^2 + c^2 - b^2}{2\,a\,c} \text{ (using cosine rule)}$$

   $$= \frac{6^2 + 3^2 - 5^2}{2 \times 6 \times 3}$$

   $$= \frac{36 + 9 - 25}{36}$$

   $$= \frac{20}{36}$$

   $$= \frac{5}{9}$$

6. 27

7. $a = 5, b = 4$

8.

   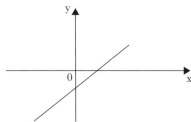

9. (a) $(x - 7)(x + 3)$

   (b) $7, -3$

   (c) $(2, -25)$

10. $\dfrac{4}{5}$

MATHEMATICS INTERMEDIATE 2 UNITS 1, 2 AND 3 PAPER 2 2011

1. $-9/10$

2. £147 900

3. $r = \sqrt{\dfrac{A}{4\pi}}$

4. (a) 106 cubic metres

   (b) 17·4 metres

5. 25·1 square metres

6. (a) (i) $\bar{x} = 41$
   (ii) $s = 2.1$

   (b) Yes, with reasons covering both conditions

7. (a) $24x + 6y = 60$

   (b) $20x + 10y = 40$

   (c) 25 points

8. $\dfrac{3}{x - 5}$

9. $\dfrac{3 - x}{x\,(x + 1)}$

10. $x = 76$ and $x = 256$

11. $0.2, 1.6$

12. 21 centimetres

13. 25·1 millimetres

14. To prove $\dfrac{\sin^2 A}{1 - \sin^2 A} = \tan^2 A$

    $$\text{Left side of equation} = \frac{\sin^2 A}{1 - \sin^2 A}$$

    $$= \frac{\sin^2 A}{\cos^2 A}$$

    $$= \tan^2 A$$

    $$= \text{right side of equation}$$

MATHEMATICS INTERMEDIATE 2 UNITS 1, 2 AND 3 PAPER 1 (NON-CALCULATOR) 2012

1. £1 158 000 000 000

2. (*a*)

mark	frequency	cumulative frequency
5	2	2
6	5	7
7	6	13
8	11	24
9	9	33
10	2	35

   (*b*) (i) 8   (ii) 7   (iii) 9

   (*c*)

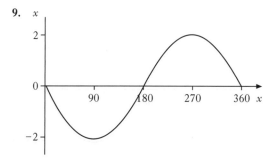

3. (*a*) A(0, 12)

   (*b*) C(3, 8)

4. $34°$

5. (*a*) 20 160

   (*b*) The median, with reason. The reason must refer to the fact that the mean is affected by one very high attendance or that the median is closer to the majority of the attendances.

6. (*a*) 2 and 4

   (*b*) A(0,8), B(2,0), C(4,0)

   (*c*) $x = 3$

7. 10 centimetres

8. (*a*) $(a + b)^2$

   (*b*) 10 000

9.

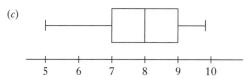

10. 2

MATHEMATICS INTERMEDIATE 2 UNITS 1, 2 AND 3 PAPER 2 2012

1. $12·5$ centimetres

2. $3x^3 + x^2 - 28x + 30$

3. 1022 mm^3

4. $-2·9, 0·6$

5. (*a*) (i) 116

      (ii) $16·33$

   (*b*) 1 and 4 (The total score is the same in both matches and in the first match the scores are more spread out.)

6. (*a*) $6x + 2y = 3148$

   (*b*) $5x + 3y = 3022$

   (*c*) Yes. The group has been overcharged by £10.

7. $\dfrac{a^2 + b^2}{ab}$

8. $36·9, 323·1$

9. $D = \sqrt{\dfrac{I}{E}}$

10. $0·4$ m

11. $\dfrac{x^5}{y^2}$

12. $75·3$ metres

13. No, $0·522 > 0·5$

14. 1

MATHEMATICS INTERMEDIATE 2 UNITS 1, 2 AND 3 PAPER 1 (NON-CALCULATOR) 2013

1. $b(6a - 7c)$

2. $y = -\dfrac{4}{3}x + 4$

3. $6\cdot28$ cm

4. $x = 4$, $y = -2$

5. $121°$

6. (a) (i) $Q_2 = 35$

   (ii) $Q_1 = 22$

   (iii) $Q_3 = 39$

   (b)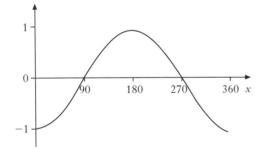

   (c) In general, the fourth year pupils spend more time on homework.
   There is less variation in the times spent on homework in fourth year than in first year.

7. $\dfrac{(x + 4)}{(x - 5)}$

8. $180°$

9. (a) $(4, 20)$

   (b) $x = 4$

10. The graph of $y = \sin(x - 90)°$ from $0°$ to $360°$

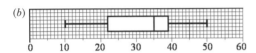

MATHEMATICS INTERMEDIATE 2 UNITS 1, 2 AND 3 PAPER 2 2013

1. $x^2 - 12x - 10$

2. 4 years because $307\,200 < 375\,000$

3.

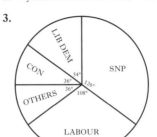

4. $30\cdot6°$

5. $x = -0\cdot4$, $x = 5\cdot4$

6. (a) (i) $\bar{x} = 82$

   (ii) $s = 3\cdot54$

   (b) mean $= 102$

   standard deviation $= 3\cdot54$

7. 14 cm

8. $b = \sqrt{\dfrac{a - c}{3}}$

9. x^3y

10. 7.6 metres

11. $\dfrac{8x + 7}{(x + 2)(x - 1)}$

12. $85\cdot4$ cm

13. 49s, 131s

MATHEMATICS INTERMEDIATE 2 UNITS 1, 2 AND 3 PAPER 1 (NON-CALCULATOR) 2014

1. $y = \dfrac{3}{4}x + 3$

2. $3x^2 - 5x - 10$

3. $\sqrt{60}$ centimetres

4. (a) (i) 0·5°C

   (ii) −3°C

   (iii) 2°C

   (b)
   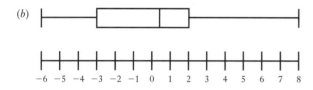

   (c) (In general) the temperatures were higher in 2014 and temperatures in 2014 were less varied.

5. $9\sqrt{10}$

6. $a = 5$

7. $a = 3,\ b = 1$

8. (a) (2, −5)

   (b) Minimum turning point

9. 18 centimetres

MATHEMATICS INTERMEDIATE 2 UNITS 1, 2 AND 3 PAPER 2 2014

1. 590

2. (a) 1180 cm³

   (b) 23 cm

3. $3(x + 4)(x - 1)$

4. (a) $3x + 2y = 4·73$

   (b) $5x + 3y = 7·52$

   (c) a loaf costs £0·85, a packet of butter costs £1·09

5. (a) (i) $\bar{x} = 56·5$

   (ii) $s = 2·4$

   (b) No, standard deviation is greater
   OR
   No, times are more spread out

6. 0·15 or 3·35

7. $r = \sqrt{\dfrac{3p}{q}}$

8. $4p^2$

9. $\dfrac{7x - 20}{x(x - 4)}$

10. because $\dfrac{25}{20} > 1$

11. (a) 84·8°

    (b) 155·2°

12. 74·3° (accept 74°)

13. 151·3 m²

Acknowledgements

Permission has been sought from all relevant copyright holders and Hodder Gibson is grateful for the use of the following:

Image © Vitalliy/Shutterstock.com (2013 Paper 2 page 8);

An image from The Highway Code © Crown Copyright. Contains public sector information licensed under the Open Government Licence v2.0 (2014 Paper 2 page 7).